# EMOTIONAL INTELLIGENCE

*MASTER YOUR EMOTIONS- RAISE YOUR EQ,*

*CRITICAL THINKING AND OPTIMIZE YOUR LIFE*

# Free Bonus: "Click The Link Below To Receive Your Free Ebooks!"

## Free Bonus "Claim Your Free eBooks" Below For Your Bonus:

## https://success321.leadpages.co/freebodymindsoul/

# TABLE OF CONTENTS

# INTRODUCTION

You know how when you are sometimes able to tell what kind of mood a person is in by looking at their expression or listening to their responses? And this does not apply only to people you already know, but even to people you just met, you can sometimes relate to them on an emotional level and respond accordingly. Well that is exactly what emotional intelligence is. It is the ability of a person to distinguish and recognize the various emotions or feelings, of not only themselves, but also those of others. Emotional intelligence also includes the ability to label these various emotions and feelings as you distinguish them and use them to guide the way you think and behave. These instincts that you have are honed so that you always have power over the situation in which you are placed. You are more capable of dealing with people and with various situations because your emotional intelligence gives you more information than those with little emotional intelligence will ever have. That gives you a lead when it comes to dealing with anyone on an emotional level.

Even though the term and concept of emotional intelligence was something that started catching the public's attention the mid-1990s, emotional intelligence in humans has always existed. But as humans, we have come a really long way 'emotionally' from where we started. And we improve emotionally as we grow up from being a baby into becoming an average adult. But in order to be a person who has mastered their emotional intelligence, you have to make sure you first understand your own emotions and why you go through them. In this book 'Emotional Intelligence: Master your emotions- Raise your EQ, critical thinking and optimize your life' I will teach you ways in which you can understand your emotions better, master them, make your life much better and reach your goals. You will learn how to handle yourself in various stressful situations and how to keep your emotions in control as well as having greater control over the situation itself because of your newly gained knowledge.

Working your way through the book, we will look at all of the facets that come into being able to take control from an emotional stance and will show you ways in which this enhances your life. When people suffer through their lack of control of emotions, it's very difficult to be happy or successful. However, emotions are not all negative especially if you are able to read them and feel empathy toward those exhibiting them. This book will show you how to use emotional intelligence to improve the way that you interact with others, thus making the path of your life a lot easier to follow.

Think of all of the circumstances in which emotions get in the way of objectivity and you will be able to see that there is always going to be some scope for improvement. This is where this book helps you to hone your instincts so that you can read situations before they become problems and that's a very powerful thing to be able to do. Entrepreneurs who have this ability will always find that they are more successful than those who prefer to wing it. Step ahead of the competition by understanding the part that emotional intelligence plays in your day to day life.

# CHAPTER ONE

---

# EMOTIONAL INTELLIGENCE – BASICS YOU NEED TO KNOW

Whether you heard about emotional intelligence from the Internet, a friend or even from a TV show, you must have rough idea about what it means. This field has gained a lot of attentions from psychologists since the late 20th century and various studies are being done on it. However, you may not realize what it isn't. This chapter will help you to put it all into perspective.

In our first chapter, we will go through the basics – what exactly emotional intelligence or EI is and how it is defined. We will then follow this with what emotional intelligence is not. People who misunderstand the meaning may believe that they have emotional intelligence, when all they really have is the ability to hide their moods. There is a huge difference.

## What is EI?

I have already explained in our introduction what emotional intelligence is. In a nutshell it compromises the ability of a person to self-evaluate themselves by their emotions and change the outcome of their behavior and thinking accordingly. Everyone has leadership skills and these leadership skills do not always mean leading a group of people; it also means the ability to lead oneself. If you know how you react when in different moods, you also know how to use that information to make your life run in a smoother way. Perhaps you work better when you are melancholy. In that case, you would use this melancholy to help you to achieve more, rather than sinking into it and doing nothing.

As technical as it may sound, your emotions can change in a matter of seconds; from sad to happy to angry and so on. But it is important that you keep your emotions in check in the long run. The way you handle your EI might vary. You may be a person who can stay angry at someone or something for a long time or you may be the exact opposite. But you can't hold on to a single emotion forever. A good balance is required to have a successful life. Therefore, you need to hone in on your moods and understand what each one of them represents. This gives you less disappointment because you know what that mood means in terms of being able to do something. Some people use anger to fire them up and give them the strength that they need to get through a task that they find difficult. They hype themselves up intentionally in order to improve their performance.

Your level of emotional intelligence is measured like this: If you are a person who has their emotions in check and knows what appropriate emotion to show at a certain circumstances and acts accordingly, then your EI level could be high. But if you are someone who cannot control their emotions and acts poorly in such circumstances, then your EI level is low. For people who fit into the latter category, they may or may not be aware of their lack of EI. But they don't have to worry since they can easily be taught to raise their EI level. People may be aware of their moods, but they may not be aware of how they affect productivity. They may also recognize the moods of others but not find it that easy to slot people into different tasks. A person with emotional intelligence will be able adjust the situation to suit the mood of a person who is working for them, so that they get maximum effort from that person, that fits with the mood that the person is in.

For some people, their EI level is naturally high. And for those who don't have a high EI, this book will tell you how to make yourself more emotionally intelligent. It is something that you can work on and observation plays a huge part in this, the first type of observation being of self.

## Various models of EI

One of the first models of EI was suggested by psychologist and science journalist Daniel Goleman. His model was a mix of the modern ability model of EI (developed in 2001 by Konstantin Vasily Pertrides) and trait model of EI (developed in 2004 by John Mayer and Peter Salovey).

In definition, the trait model of emotional intelligence encompasses 'behavioral dispositions and self-perceived abilities'. It follows the pattern of one's behavior and the skillset one uses to navigate their way through life. It can be measured through self-report'. The ability model of emotional intelligence focuses on a person's singular ability to analyze emotional information, process it individually and then use this emotional understanding to negotiate the social environment that they are a part of and that they can contribute to.

## Why is EI important?

People with low emotional intelligence or EQ (Emotional quotient) tend to lack communicative skills, which is one of the most important traits in human beings since we are social creatures. We live in a society where communicating properly with each other is mandatory in order to lead a successful life. But in order to communicate, a person has to be able to express his or her emotions properly while simultaneously being able to understand, process and navigate the emotional standing of the people he or she is communicating with. Without this dual understanding, proper communication will fail and it will give rise to conflict.   So it is absolutely necessary a person has a good EQ. Having a high EQ helps build relationships easier, show empathy toward other people because they themselves go through the same emotions. It is also important to know that the comfortable EQ level varies with each person.

## So what is the point of emotional intelligence?

It is emotional intelligence that will make you see things in a different manner to those that do not possess it. Someone who has emotional intelligence will be able to understand their employees in a better manner and be able to allot certain work to those that he/she knows will be able to meet deadlines. It's not just a matter of knowing their work ability. If their minds are not on the job – and this can change considerably depending upon their emotions – then they will not be able to perform in the same way as they would if their emotional state was different.

# What emotional intelligence is not

Emotional intelligence is not about being able to hide your emotions. It is not about being able to ignore the emotions of others and put them to one side, thinking that they are not relevant to the task at hand. It isn't about knowing when to hand out the handkerchief or when to be sympathetic. It's all about knowing how the emotions affect the way that a person reacts to a given stimulus. Give a nervous and upset man the task of standing in front of an audience, and the chances are that he will fail no matter how much encouragement you give him. However, choose that same person in a mood that is positive and the speech is likely to be a lot more successful. We are all capable of much more than we give ourselves credit for, but emotions often get in the way of the way that we perform. Thus, knowing those limitations and recognizing them helps you to be able to put square pegs in square holes and run life in a much smoother way. People who avoid certain tasks do so because they feel uncomfortable with them. However, if the emotions are gaged to enjoy the work, there will be less evasion of that work. Thus, someone with emotional intelligence will be able to work around the emotions of others – not be ignoring them – but by being aware of them and knowing how that particular person will react to any given task under those particular circumstances when emotions are getting in the way of logical reason.

Many people throw themselves into work as a means to avoid emotions. The kind of work that they are given should depend upon how they will perform and people with emotional intelligence will recognize this. For example, someone who has suffered loss may be feeling empty and very emotional, but may want to bury themselves in work to get away from that loss. In circumstances such as this, the emotionally intelligent boss would be able to give them bulk work which would suit the purpose but which will not make them feel more emotional. They will know how to gage what the employee is capable of and adjust their workload to take account of this. It is more than empathy although empathy plays a part in it because empathy – or putting yourself in someone else's shoes – will help you to understand the mood that the person is in and the kind of workload that particular person is capable of dealing with given the state of mind that they are in. Someone with emotional intelligence will also have a much better approach to people and will be able to recognize from facial expressions and bodily gestures the kind of reception they are likely to get from people they come into contact with. This is helpful from many different points of view.

# CHAPTER TWO

# WHAT EMOTIONAL INTELLIGENCE IS ALL ABOUT

Since we have covered the basic definition of emotional intelligence, we can now move on to the main steps that make up emotional intelligence. In this chapter, I will talk about all the mental steps that make up to a good emotional intelligence or understanding of the psych.

## Knowing

This step is basically knowing or perceiving what the people around you or what the people you are trying to communicate with are feeling. Whether you understand the emotion or not, just knowing what the emotion is will help you give appropriate responses up to a certain level.

For example, if the person you are communicating with seems to be sad for a specific reason, you need to immediately understand their emotion; but knowing that he or she is sad will help you respond accordingly at that moment. Some people struggle at perceiving emotions and there is some amount of effort required from them. But most of us can easily recognize what the other person is feeling and what emotion they are experiencing by looking at the way they speak (tone of voice), their body language, their expressions, the words they use etc.

One of the biggest mistakes that people without emotional intelligence make is the assumption that emotions do not come into work performance. They do. Some people are very capable of taking on a larger workload in a certain mood and that mood makes them more productive. Others may be given a job and will prevaricate because they are not confident and their mood stops them from wanting to do that job. Thus, someone who is emotionally intelligent will know by the mood displayed which work is more suited to the individual and be able to work in a more efficient manner because of his/her emotional intelligence.

## Understanding

All of us have gone through the basic emotions such as happiness, sadness, anger, fear and so on. But as I said, these emotions are just the basics and they evolve into a complex of specific emotions which are complicated. So even if we know what emotion the other person is going through it is important that we understand what that emotion means, particularly for that individual.

For people with low EQ, not being able to understand an emotion even if they know what it is will be a problem, since they will not respond in the right way. For example, if a person with a low EQ is communicating with another person who is going through fear, they may not respond accordingly. Because even though he or she knows that the emotion is fear, he or she does not understand the emotion exactly and may respond with more fear or an inappropriate emotional response and the both of them are now not comfortable. If you respond to a stimulus in an inappropriate manner, you don't get better results. In fact, you alienate people and show how little empathy you have. This doesn't bide well for making relationships work or getting any positive outcome from a given situation.

Instead of doing this, if this person with a low EQ is taught how to understand emotions better, he or she will respond to fear with reassurance and optimism or any other appropriate response depending upon the recipient and the level of fear. However, for some people, understanding emotions does not come easily and they have to put in a lot of effort in order to start understanding the emotions that other people go through. Those that work with the emotional may have high emotional intelligence, or they may simply respond in the way that they are taught to respond. An example here would be working on a help line. Not everyone that answers the telephone will have a good level of emotional intelligence. They will simply answer queries in the way they are taught to and may feel no empathy toward the person on the other end of the line. However, if you have ever telephoned a help line or worked in a help line environment, those who do have emotional intelligence will stand out as being more helpful to those in need of that help because not only will they give the official line, they will know something about listening and mirroring thoughts to help those with emotional blocks. Those blocks will not be seen by those with low emotional intelligence. I give this example because in a case where you are talking on a telephone, you don't have the presence of another person to judge. There is no body language. There is no facial expression and yet there are those who excel in this type of work simply because of their own ability to use their emotional intelligence to grasp what the emotions are of the person on the other end of the line.

## Reasoning

Reasoning is just as important as the other steps. Reasoning helps you to relate to the emotions of the other person and generate your own response. Sometimes reasoning might have to occur before you can understand an emotion. It may take time for you to truly understand or comprehend the depth of the emotion; reasoning on the other hand, is more logical. If you could figure out why the person is feeling the way they are, you could respond to them accordingly. This comprehension of why is not necessarily understanding the emotion itself; it can, in a way, be seen as the difference between sympathy and empathy. While you may not truly understand the emotion fully, you can respond to them because you are sympathetic. And this sympathy requires a definite EQ. However, if you have emotional intelligence, your empathy factor will set you apart from those with lower emotional intelligence.

A person with low EQ might not be able to reason properly with another person's emotion. For example, they can aggravate an already aggravated situation. Instead, if they developed their EQ they can reason properly with the other person's emotion and respond calmly. Learning to reason will help a person respond better and more appropriately. Someone with high emotional intelligence will know how to respond to given circumstances and will use their emotional intelligence to make the situation easier not only for themselves but for others who are involved in whatever conflict arises.

# Managing

Managing emotions properly is the final step to achieving a high EQ. But it is no less important than the others. Because even if you can perceive, understand and reason with the emotions of another person, if you fail to have understand and manage your own emotions, you will have failed at proper communication. This is because managing your emotions also means managing the consequences of your emotions. Every situation demands a particular course of action; if you can't manage your own emotional response and act accordingly, then you end up hurting those around you and yourself. It is easy for anyone to act or say things without thinking or keeping their emotions under control. It is the ability to know what to say, when to say it and where to say it. Thus, knowing your emotions and how they affect your performance is very helpful at increasing your emotional intelligence. In a later chapter, we will show you how to do this because diary entries can help you to see where your emotions take you and this helps you to respond in a more intelligence manner that ups the ante and makes it possible for people to work through their emotional blockages in a way that causes no friction.

Let's say you are in a professional environment and there is discussion about something that you do not like. If you are person with a high EQ, you will manage your emotions and respond accordingly and keeping things professional. But someone with a low EQ who is incapable of comprehending and managing their own emotional will say something inappropriate and create a bad atmosphere where they hurt themselves. So it is absolutely important that you know to manage your emotions and control them.    There is a great difference between being able to control your emotions and being able to totally understand them to the extent that you can use them to make a situation better.   When you have a high level of emotional intelligence, you are able to adjust your way of thinking to fit different circumstances and this makes you a lot more capable than the employer who does not have any notion about the way that people's minds work.

# CHAPTER THREE

# THE IMPORTANCE OF EI OR EQ

If I haven't already emphasized on how extremely important EQ is for our everyday functioning, then I will elaborate more in our third chapter.

The term 'emotional intelligence' made its first appearance in a paper that was written by a man who went by the name of Michael Beldoch. This paper was published in the year 1964, and was later followed by another paper in the year 1966, entitled 'Emotional Intelligence and Emancipation', written by another man named B. Leuner. And it was around this time that EQ started getting the attention of psychologists around the world. Soon they started realizing that EQ is much more efficient at predicting a person's actions and success than IQ. It also resulted in the overall satisfaction and happiness of an individual. It wasn't a measure of how intelligent a person is from an academic point of view, but how intelligent they are from the point of view of being able to act in accordance with emotions.

Therefore, we must understand that no matter what our IQ might be, emotional intelligence is very important in order for us to become better people in our society. It helps us become more aware, understanding and empathetic of other people's circumstances and emotions, it helps us to manage our own emotions better and achieve our goals faster.

I will elaborate and explain how EQ is important in the various aspects of our life.

## Mentally

Since emotions are a mental aspect, it is easily understood how much EQ affects our mental health. Even people with social anxiety can have a good mental health if they improve their EQ. People will low EQ become easily mentally drained as they do not know how to manage their emotions properly. By improving the state of our mental health through proper management of our EQ, we can live a happier life and have a more positive outlook toward our future and the way things are around us. And at the same time, achieve all our goals.

The mind is a very powerful thing. You may have heard of the "Laws of Attraction" and how if someone believes sufficiently in something, it can happen. That's the power of the mind. You can also look at things such as the placebo effect because the power of the mind to heal is incredible. If you were to believe that you were seriously ill, then it's unlikely that you could really work toward feeling better because the underlying belief will stop you. However, if you believe that a placebo works to make you feel better, then you must also accept that the power of the mind is vast. Knowing your own emotions and being able to adjust them or use them to your benefit instead of your detriment is very powerful indeed and will improve the way that you look at life and how you see the world around you.

## Physically

Even though EQ is all about emotions and how we manage them, our emotions have a physical impact on our bodies. Stress has a huge impact on our body and if we don't take steps toward stress management, then it will eventually take a big toll on our overall health and well being. Our body and our mind are not separate; they are connected to each other quite deeply. You can learn to understand and manage your own emotional intelligence by keeping an eye on your body. Even if you don't realize it, your body reacts to each emotion in specific ways; pick up on these physical cues and it will be easy for you to manage your EQ. For example:

• Stress may make you feel like you have a knot in your tummy, heaviness in your chest or quick breathing

• When you are sad, you may end up feeling like your entire body is too heavy; you literally feel weighed down by the world. Your limbs are too tired to move and you feel a sense of slowness overall.

• On the other hand, happiness may make you feel extra energetic; butterflies are jumping in your stomach and your heart maybe beating a mile a minute, even as you can't seem to stop smiling.

A person with a low EQ will not know how to manage stress or anger and may take it out on their bodies. They deal with such emotions by over eating or starving or even hurting themselves physically in case of anger or sorrow. So it is extremely important that we manage our emotions and keep our bodies healthy. The other thing that you need to understand is that people hide a multiplicity of emotions within their physical state of health. The pains that they are experiencing may not represent bodily injury or illness but may just be as a result of a stressed mind needing an outlet to justify the state of mind that the individual is in. People in unhappy circumstances, for example, may become dramatic about illnesses that they don't actually have, but to them, they are very real. This may be their way of explaining why they are negative in emotions rather than facing up to the real reasons.

Conversely, there are others that use their emotions to actually get things moving. A writer, who is aware that he writes better fiction when he is sad would choose times of sadness to be at his most creative. An artist who knows that emotions fire the imagination and that produces better artwork under this kind of stress would be able to use that to produce better work. It's the same in any working situation because the person with emotional intelligence will be able to gage their emotions and use them to become more productive. For example, a decorator may do a better job when his mind is filled with emotions that are reflective. It works in different ways for different jobs though the emotionally intelligent will know how to make the most of their emotions to succeed.

## Relationships

Relationships are a major part of our everyday lives. Having a high emotional intelligence quotient will help you navigate all your relationships more easily; both your personal and your professional lives will see a definite improvement. When you understand your emotions and then learn how to deal with them, it becomes easier for you to relate to other people and empathize with them and their emotional needs.

When you are able to empathize – and remember that means putting yourself in someone else's shoes – you can gage what they can do to be at their most productive and help them to get beyond negative emotions. Thus, you will understand the intricacies of a relationship better if you are emotionally intelligent.

Stay focused on what is happening now. When you are able to let go of old grudges and resentments, you will find that the present situation is easier to handle. If you do meet someone against whom you could potentially hold a grudge, having a high EQ will make it easier for you to resolve those old disagreements and feelings. It goes without saying that resolving a conflict makes both parties happy; this way you can react according to their emotions and it will help you lead a happier life because the people around you are happy.

Emotionally intelligent people are aware of themselves. They know how their reactions affect those around them and thus are more likely to make long term friendships. Their positive attitude and their ability to listen to others and actually take notice of what they hear will be sufficient to encourage friendships and to make the most of colleagues in whatever situation they find themselves. Someone with emotional intelligence can handle difficult situations with people and still come out of the other side of those situations with the same level of positivity. They are more objective. They understand the needs of others and that places them in a very good position to have a career which is in a position of high standing.

## Resolving Conflicts

Doesn't it feel great when you realize or know that you avoided or resolved a fight or a conflict because your emotions were in check? That is exactly what improving your EQ does to your responsive skills in such situation. Given that you are able to comprehend what the other person feels and you are well aware of their mindset and their perception of the world, you will be able to respond to them accordingly in a moment of conflict or disagreement. This way, you can avoid any undue bitterness or resentment from cropping up. This will also help the other person relate to you better. Here are some pointers as to what you can do when you are faced with conflict. You will find these helpful in your journey through life, no matter how great or small that conflict is.

• Choose your arguments. It will definitely take time and energy, but when you argue your point from a rational perspective instead of randomly yelling and fighting it out, you will be able to actually resolve an issue, or at the very least, agree to disagree. Such positive resolutions will help your relationships stay intact.

• Choose your moment. Often people with less emotional intelligence do not make the most of their situations and choose the wrong time to bring up subjects that would otherwise have a more positive response. When you are able to use your emotional intelligence to time any conflict, you can gage the emotional state of the person with whom the conflict will occur and choose a time when it is likely to have the least negative impact.

- Learn to forgive any hurtful behavior that people have displayed in the past towards you. The natural instinct is to want to punish or to seek revenge against them for causing you that hurt. Not only does this not resolve the conflict, it can potentially worsen as it becomes a tit-for-tat game. Instead, let it go and focus on either resolving the issue or simply putting it to rest.

- Bring an end to those conflicts that have no visible resolution. You cannot have a solution to every problem; as stated before, just agree to disagree. It takes two people to continue an argument. You can choose to back off instead of constantly arguing your point further, even if you cannot come to an agreement.

## Leadership

As I mentioned earlier, leadership does not only mean leading group of people, but also leading yourself. If you have mastered the steps to improving your EQ, leadership becomes an easy task. People tend to look up to a person who understands them and connects with them on a personal level. So understanding other people's emotions and reacting positively makes you a good leader. Also, when the people around you look at how in control you are of yourself and your emotions, the will automatically visualize you as a good leader they can learn from. These skills help you team become stronger as a group and as individuals because you now have a bond with each one of them.

## Learning to trust

Often people in high places are unable to delegate because their emotional attachment to certain jobs will not let them. If you have emotional intelligence, you will be able to gage who is suited to the tasks that are at hand. That means that people around you will develop their skills quicker and will become more productive, freeing you up to pursue new ideas. That's one of the most important attributes of emotionally intelligent people and examples can be given of people who do this. When you speak to entrepreneurs such as Richard Branson, he says that when he delegates work to someone else, it's because he knows that they are capable of doing that work and that he no longer has to take up room in his head with those jobs, freeing him up to think of even more inventive things.

## Achieving Goals

All of us have goals that we want to accomplish in life. These goals can be professional, social and personal. And they need not always be long term goals. Because we can have short term goals as well, like burning 300 calories every day or making sure you eat vegetables with at least one meal per day.   Achieving any of these goals becomes a lot easier if we improve our EQ. In case of your long term goals and their success, it is important that you keep a positive attitude and the only way to do that is to improve your EQ levels. If your EQ is high, then it means you are in control of your emotions; which in turn will make you more confident. And with confidence you can overcome minor setbacks and achieve your everyday goals as well, thus improving further. The law of attraction works in much the same way. It is your belief in yourself, in your capabilities and in your goals that helps you to reach them. Coaches all over the world are teaching people to change their mindsets and stop limiting themselves because at the end of the day, the only real limitation in your life is the chain of your thoughts. If you do not believe that you can achieve, it's more likely that you will fail.

We may never really fully understand emotional intelligence. But we can make sure that with what we do understand, we can improve our lives personally, socially and professionally. So now you understand how important emotional intelligence is in our everyday life. And as we progress in life, we need to always try improving our EQ. In following chapters, we will show you exercises that you can do to help you to improve you EQ. Getting your emotions in check is one of them and although you may find that some of the exercises seem a little away from the topic, they are related. The reason for the relationship between these activities and you success in gaining emotional intelligence is that you maximize the potential by becoming more in tone between your mind and body and these exercises also help you to do that.

People are beginning to see the benefits of mindfulness. They are beginning to see that there is more to meditation than simply switching off your mind. All of these activities help you to be able to be more empathetic toward others and this in turn raises your level of emotional intelligence as far as relationships go. You are also made much more aware of your own weaknesses and can strengthen up areas where you know that your emotional intelligence is letting you down.

People who like who they are can use their contentment to help them to see why others may not be as happy and content with their circumstances. This empathy is so important to emotional intelligence because if you are unable to see the emotions of others and how they affect their decision making processes, you are liable to fail as any kind of leader because you lack empathy.

# CHAPTER FOUR

# EXERCISES TO IMPROVE YOUR EMOTIONAL INTELLIGENCE

**A** lot of people underestimate what they are capable of doing. If you were presented with a new job, you have several different approaches that you can take. You can exhibit fear which will make you very cautious in your approach. You can exhibit confidence which can make you careless. There is a cross section of emotions that come into play every time that you are faced with a new task that needs to be done. Perhaps the following case scenarios will hit a chord with you as they may be things that you have had to do in your life:

- Passing a driving test

- Buying a new home

- Being faced with having to look after a sick pet

- Being faced with the death of a family member

- Being faced with the breakup of a relationship

There could be thousands of other scenarios that you may have been faced with during the course of your life. For example, you may be asked to do something you have never done before and your emotions go into overdrive when this happens. If you have a high level of emotional intelligence, you can prepare for these events and probably will have.

In the case of passing your driving test, you know what state of mind you need to be in to drive well. Perhaps you need to be driving for an hour before the test so that you are relaxed with the car function and feel fairly relaxed with the situation of driving. Someone who is very nervous will probably make mistakes. However, emotional intelligence will tell you that all the examiner wants is half an hour of comfortable driving that shows that you are capable of acting safely in set circumstances. When you are able to change your mindset to think of the driving test in these simple terms, you are also able to control your emotions so that you don't see the task as an emotional one.

When you are faced with purchasing a new home for the first time, you may be a little nervous about it. Perhaps your fear stems from not knowing how you will cope with all of the bills that will be involved in the purchase of the house or whether you can get the cash freed up in time for the purchase date. Perhaps you don't know enough about buildings to have confidence in your level of expertise and may be very nervous about this new experience. People with emotional intelligence will approach it in a very detailed way which lists all the pros and cons and doesn't allow the emotions to go into overdrive. They will have everything planned. They will have been able to gage the emotions of the person selling the house and may even have used this to give them the power that they need to reduce the price on a basis that will be accepted by the seller. People with less emotional intelligence may just make an offer and not think of the way that this will be perceived by the seller. The emotionally intelligent person will justify any drop in price and be ready with lots of logical reasons that will make the seller see that it's common sense that he must reduce his price.

When you have to look after a sick pet and have no experience of what to do, it can throw you. People with emotional intelligence will know how to deal with it. In fact, they excel in unforeseen circumstances and are able to overcome their own doubts by simply getting on with the job at hand. They don't let their emotions get in the way of what is needed. Even if the pet has to be put down, they are able to justify this in their minds and their acceptance levels will be better than for those who think with their emotions rather than with their head.

I am using examples like that because they are things that people react to in different ways. In the case of death, it's always going to be sad. If you dealing with people who have lost someone and understand the intricacies of loss, you are better able to deal with treating them in the right way. Thus, when you go through loss, are you emotionally intelligent and able to reach acceptance levels? Or are you someone who lets those emotional levels affect your performance in life in general?

A breakup in the relationship that you have can also send you some real curve balls. Those with little emotional intelligence may get to the stage where they are unable to function because the emotions take priority over life. They may not feed themselves. They may not do all the things that they should do. They may miss work or become very withdrawn. It may just take a while for emotional intelligence to be able to come through because the negative experience is taking priority in their minds.

The reason we are showing you different case scenarios is you need to keep a diary and write down your feelings and note the kind of things that you were able to do faced with those feelings. Some people are geared by negative situations and in order to make themselves more positive, surround themselves with work of some kind or another that allows them to keep their emotions in check. If you find that you are efficient when going through emotional events, write it down. You need to learn all about you. When you take the time to examine why you feel angry and what it does to your performance levels, you get to know your own strengths and weaknesses and can adjust them to suit different situations. For example, if you can give a talk in front of a hundred people even though you fear giving that talk, examine the things that you do to lessen the anxiety because these will help you with other tasks. Write down what it is that you fear and what you did to overcome it and remember to note the emotions that you were feeling while this was happening.

By keeping a diary of your moods and of what you achieved, you are able to see a pattern emerge. If you think of the following as the types of emotions that may fuel your activities, then you can write down what you were able to achieve when you were in that state of mind:

Anger, fear, sadness, happiness, euphoria, nostalgia, depression, anxiety

Each of these fears and many more besides make up what fires you into doing things within your life and by understanding them, you are able to also understand what emotions do what to your way of thinking or your motivation levels. Emotionally intelligent people are able to do this automatically, but if you want to improve your emotional intelligence, then observation is a very good way to do it.

**Learn not to interrupt what is happening around you**

Often, people who are opinionated tend to try to finish other people's conversations. They feel frustration and they interrupt others but you may not be getting a clear picture of someone else's emotional intelligence or even your own if you are in the habit of doing this. Try to work out what it is that makes you interrupt and try and distance yourself from a situation rather than doing it because you cause all kinds of different emotions to happen when you do this. Giving yourself a little time away from a situation helps you to gage your response to any given stimuli in a much more intelligent manner. For example, if someone is shouting at you, it can be very tempting to shout back and you may just begin saying things that you later regret. By placing yourself in an empathetic frame of mind, you can diminish that anger and emotionally intelligent people will do this, giving them space to work out a way to explain something in a manner that is more acceptable to the recipient. The next time that you find yourself interrupting something, try not to. Step away and then examine your emotions. The emotions are something that rise and lower all of the time. They are ever changing. You can't take back words that you have said, though if you allow your emotions to calm before you speak, you may save yourself a lot of hassle and a lot of time and save face.

## Look out for connections

This is something that I do all of the time. In the past, I would never bother with doing this but what I have found since I started exercising my level of emotional intelligence is that it always pays to look for connections. Connection between two human beings is what brings them together into a space of agreement and empathy. If you can connect with the emotions that you are feeling when in the company of people, you can begin to see that certain types of people bring out different connections. If you can then work out a way so that your mind connects with theirs, often you can overcome difficulties that would otherwise be hard to overcome.

For example, when I wanted to buy a car, I didn't have quite enough for the old car that I wanted. The owner was very proud of the car and although he knew the worth of the car, he also knew what he held as emotional value on the car. I was able to pick this up during our conversation. By switching my tactics and playing on the fact that I too had an emotional connection with this car in the same way as he did, he was prepared to lower the price, knowing that the car was going to someone who would love it in the same way as he did and that, to him, was more important than the financial aspect of the situation.

In another situation in the workplace, the connection I found between a reluctant junior and myself was that she had really tried hard in the past to advance her career. People simply didn't let her get very far. It was more important to them that she did all the tasks that no one else really wanted to do. She was not learning new things and although she was useful as a junior, it was obvious that we would lose her services if people continued to treat her in this way. We talked about the potential of training. I could feel her negative vibes toward me as her senior. All the seniors she had ever had were condescending and had given her work that was only fit for a junior and she had no trust in the situation. I asked how she would feel to be given a set number of hours each week for this training to advance her career. I also talked to our immediate boss in private and spoke about the value that I thought she had for the company who were not really giving her a chance. He was in agreement that we could train her and that she should be used for less mundane tasks. It took a while for her to trust me, but when she did, the response that I got was amazing. Not only did she want to learn, but she actually achieved much more than she had thought possible and people around you can if you are able to use your emotional intelligence to bring the best out of them and can find some connection point between you. The connection between me and her was that both wanted careers, were both willing to try and at some stage in both of our lives had experienced being held back by others.

## Learning all about your inner feelings

This may sound a little strange, but have you ever been emotional about something and not really understood what the emotions are all about? Many people do. For example, they may feel reticence of they may feel some sense of apprehension but may not know where this is coming from. Meditation will help you to connect to your inner thoughts and that is covered in the next chapter, but for now, make a diary note when you are feeling apprehensive about things within your life and try and work out why you feel that way. Associate your emotions with the way that you react to a given stimuli. I wanted a new house but was very afraid and very stressed when my offer was accepted. I examined why and what I found was that my mind was not that comfortable with the unknown. Knowing that, I was able to make myself more familiar with the house in question and make it more familiar to me, so that it was no longer the unknown. If you can understand why you are feeling reticent about things, you can also work on the level of your prevarication or your lack of motivation and this is very useful from a work life and personal life point of view.

# Try tuning in with people you know

Sometimes to bring out the best in your emotional intelligence you need to have an opinion from someone who cares about you and who is able to discuss the turmoil that you mind is facing. If you have someone that you can trust to discuss these things with it really does help you to understand where all of these emotions are coming from and sometimes you can't see the reasoning yourself. There is a very good system that psychologists use to mirror the emotions of clients so that they see them in a clearer way and by getting the input from someone who knows you well, you may find that the answers to your dilemmas are easier to understand and to deal with.

One woman that I know suffered terribly stomach pains. She had nothing wrong with her and asked me why I thought she was having them. Her husband was suffering from cancer. We talked about things for a long time and it became more and more obvious to me why these stomach aches were occurring. Her emotional knots regarding her husband's illness were taking their toll on her body. While she had nothing physically wrong, she wasn't looking after herself as well as she could have been. She was emotionally eating. She was not taking her time to eat or taking much notice of the types of food she was eating. In fact, she had given up listening to her body altogether. When people do this, they lose track of their reality and can develop all kinds of problems which are signs of other things happening inside them. When these thoughts were mirrored back at her and it was explained that she needed to stay strong for her husband, she began to prioritize in a different way, concentrating on making her own emotions and bodily condition better so that she was better able to help her husband when he needed it. These blockages occur for several reasons and you may find that people you work with have similar blockages. Empathy toward them will help them to understand and if you are suffering unnecessarily because of emotions that you have in your life you do need to be able to listen to all of the signals that your body is giving you.

## Knowing when to let go

This is another thing that you can get to grips with on your own. If you have things in your mind that stop you from progressing, chances are that you are ruminating on them a little too much. You need to understand that there are different things in life that need different approaches. The things you can do nothing to change need to be let go of. You will be surprised just how effective this is. Although your mind may be filled with a huge idea of dissatisfaction about something, if it's something you can do nothing about, let it go. You free up your intelligence to use in other directions.

One man that came for help with handling his emotional intelligence had a blockage because he had a neighbor who annoyed him to the point of anger. The neighbor was never going to change the way that he was and he was there first. However, this man had a fixation about the state of the neighbor's garden and the way that the neighbor's approach to life was so different from his own. This was something he could do nothing about. He was taught to let go of this negative feeling because it solved nothing and although it was hard for him to do at first, he eventually managed to tell himself that it wasn't worth pursuing.

When he stopped worrying about it, he actually took time to get to know the neighbor over the course of years and found out that the neighbor was actually a very nice person but that he had different priorities. He was amazed at the ability of the man to produce the most stunning art and sculpture. The moment he let go of his negativity toward the neighbor, his life became much easier and when this priority was taken out of his mind, he actually found that he enjoyed the quirky nature of the man next door and that part of him was jealous because he had never been able to do the things in his life that he wanted to do. He had always been weighed down by obligation. The man next door taught him to be more accepting of the things you cannot change and this enriched his emotional intelligence.

# CHAPTER FIVE

# LEARNING TO MEDITATE AND HOW IT HELPS EMOTIONAL INTELLIGENCE

You may not be aware of it, but meditation gives you more control over your emotional responses to given stimuli, especially if you add mindfulness to the picture. The idea of mindfulness is to observe all of the facets of your life and learn not to judge them. That means if you are sitting in a garden, don't think about the negative things about that garden. Appreciate what is there. See the cup as half full. Yes, you may be able to think of improvements that you can make to the garden but see these are potential improvements rather than correcting something which is wrong. It's a kind of acceptance of what is happening around you and people's stress levels often stand in the way of this kind of objectivity.

If you meditate, you get to learn about the connection between the mind and the body and have much more control over the kind of life that you live. You are much less inclined to be stressed and will learn to breathe in the correct way. You will find that your mind is calmer and that you are able to feel more empathy toward others than you currently do. This empathy will help you to exercise emotional intelligence toward others and that means making better friendships and forging stronger working relationships with those who are around you.

In business circles there is a big push these days toward people understanding all about neuro linguistic programming which is seeing things from other people's perspective and thus being able to gage business dealings in a more positive way. Meditation helps you to start to focus your mind on the kind of practice coupled with mindfulness because what you learn from it is a very good sense of observation both of external things and also you get a much better sense of self, meaning that you don't let your emotions control your state of mind or your abilities.

There are many more comprehensive books available on meditation but basically the steps that you take are to get away from the noise and hustle of the world to a space where you are peaceful and to sit in a certain pose while concentrating on your breathing. This pose is usually sitting on a cushion with your knees bent and your ankles crossed. The reason that a cushion is used is to help give your back a little more support and to make your legs more comfortable. Practitioners of meditation usually sit in what is known as the "Lotus" position but this is too hard for people who have not had sufficient practice.

If you choose to use a dining chair, this is okay too because there are no rules with meditation that you have to be on a cushion. As long as you are centered on what you are doing, a chair is fine. You place your hands so that you are grounded. On a cushion, your hands would be placed onto your knees with the palms upward and your thumbs and middle fingers touching while on a chair, you would place your strongest hand palm upward onto your knee and then place the other hand into it. Your feet, in the case of the chair position, would be flat on the floor.

The atmosphere for your meditation should be airy and calm. There should be no outside distractions. You need to learn to breathe in the correct way. Breathe in through your nostrils to the count of 7 and hold the breath for the count of 3 before exhaling to the count of eight. If you are breathing correctly, your upper abdomen makes a pivoting motion. So practice this first before you think of meditating. When you have the rhythm of your breathing correct, keep breathing in this way and close your eyes. Your concentration should only be on the breathing aspect. See your breathing as a positive energy entering your body, let it stay inside for a moment and then breathe out - counting to one. All the time that you are doing this, you should think of nothing else at all. Breathe in through the nostrils, count, breathe out and then count to two and so forth until you reach ten. Then do the same thing again.

In the early stages of meditation, what you find is that you mind is distracted. This is because the mind is accustomed to working and you are not accustomed to thinking about nothing. However, it's important that you achieve this. Little by little, with daily practice of about fifteen minutes, well-spaced out from meals, you will find that you are more and more capable of putting thoughts to one side during the meditation.

You will also find that this action will bring down your blood pressure and lower your heart rate, so at the end of meditation, you should never stand up and go about your everyday activities without using the period between meditation and movement to assess how you have done with your meditation.

## How meditation helps your emotional intelligence

The way that meditation helps emotional intelligence is that it helps you to be more in control of your life. That space of time that you give your subconscious to work is like adding REM sleep to your everyday life and that's a very valuable thing. You may not know it, but during the course of your sleep, the REM period allows the subconscious to heal itself and in fact when you wake up in the morning with great thoughts, these are because your subconscious has been working on your mental thoughts and coming up with solutions during your sleep. You may find that this happens after you meditate as well. The clarity of your mind unclutters it and allows your emotions a little bit of space from negative thought or leftover thoughts from the day so you are much more in control of your emotions and also very much aware of them. If you are aware of your emotions and are noting them down as I explained in the last chapter, you are increasing the potential of your emotional intelligence, but you shouldn't stop there. Use all the lessons that you learn to improve your own sense of emotional intelligence in looking at your own life, but use mindfulness to help you when you try to acknowledge the emotions of others.

## How mindfulness works

When you practice mindfulness, you tell yourself that this moment in time may be all that you have. The past has gone so you drop that from your line of thinking. The future has not yet arrived, so does not form part of the equation. Observe life, observe people but learn that you do not have the right to pass judgment. Observation makes your mind very rich and helps you to feel empathy instead of the potential negative feelings you may otherwise have felt.

Mindfulness means listening to people instead of being so busy that you don't have time to listen to them. You do need to practice this to up your emotional intelligence because you cannot empathize if you can't even be bothered to listen to people around you and empathy is a huge part of emotional intelligence. When you can actually put yourself in someone else's situation, you are able to judge things in a better way. The boss that can understand the negative impact an employee may have if placed in a certain circumstance will be much more aware of the potential of negative impact. Thus, he will choose other work for that negative person that is something they can excel at without having that same negative impact.

Mindfulness means looking after your body and being aware of everything you are doing and with emotional intelligence this is quite important. If you are too busy to self-observe, you learn nothing about how your emotions affect a given situation. If you make the time to observe the times when you excel, you also know which emotions spurred you on and can use those emotions when you need motivation to do a lot of work. Thus, observe people around you but distance yourself sufficiently not to judge them. Learn to listen and learn to be humble. It will help you to be able to gage other people's intelligence and how it is affecting their performance

# CHAPTER SIX

# EMOTIONAL INTELLIGENCE IN YOUR SOCIAL LIFE

As I said earlier, humans are social creatures. We live in a 'society', which means that all of us have social life. To improve your social impact, it is important that you have a good level of EQ and emotional intelligence. This allows you to interact with others in a seamless kind of way, so that your life compliments that of the lives of the people who cross your path. You may be surprised at how much impact your emotional intelligence has on others but believe me, it has. Your attitude toward people is essential if you want to increase your emotional intelligence.

In this chapter, we are going to focus on how to improve and use your EQ properly in your social life.

## Listening

It is the most crucial part of your social endeavors. 'Do for others what you wish them to do for you' – remember this saying so that you know how much listening to other people is important. It is not until you learn to comprehend your own emotions that you realize how much you want the people around you to be able to understand you. And when you realize that you want them to do that, you will also understand that giving back is just as important as receiving this sort of sympathy is. So always make sure you hear out other people when and try to get an understanding of what their emotions are.

Because when you are only focused on your own emotions and how you want to express them, people around you will eventually lose interest in you and in what you have to say. Listening to others will give you a perspective of their lives and of ways you can interact with them. When you listen, you can empathize with them and the communication between you becomes much easier. Also, empathizing with other people will keep your emotions in check and it will make you feel grateful for the thing you have in life.

A powerful tool for increasing your emotional intelligence, listening is vital to all of the relationships that you make during the course of your life. Many people make their opinion well known to all around them. They may even have opinions about things they know nothing about and what message this sends to others is that they are not someone worth listening to. You must know people like this. Don't follow their lead. Even if you know more than others, you should never use that fact to put the importance of what other people have to say into a lower priority than hearing your own voice.

Often people who are loud in their opinions are not particularly successful in their lives and are using loudness to try to cover up the fact that success seems to be eluding them. The fact is that people who are not empathetic and who place more importance on self than on what others have to say suffer emotionally. They are unable to look at their emotions in any kind of educational way because they believe they already have the answers and are not open to learning anything new. If you find yourself doing this, try to stop yourself because by doing so, you may open up channels to up your emotional intelligence and read people in a better way. You may even find that you are better able to make relationships that are lasting and that are two ways. Being an active listener helps you to empathize and helps you to see how other people's emotions work and that's the other side of emotional intelligence – being able to use your own sensitivity to others to help read them correctly. That way, you open up the possibility of advancing in your workplace and gaining promotion. People who don't listen are often passed over when it comes to promotion because in all managerial positions, listening forms an integral part of working with people.

## Speak Without Over Thinking

We live in a free world where we are allowed to express our own opinions. You should never be afraid to say something you believe in or strongly feel about. If you over think the things that you are going to say to people, then the moment to express what you wanted to would have passed on. However, never speak out of turn with anger and negative emotions in your mind. Social situations mostly mean that you are with your own circle of friends. Don't ever be afraid to say what you think; your opinion is your own and you are entitled to it. And you must do it with confidence, because when you do, people around you will see you as a confident and honest person and they will respect you for that. The problem with speaking without thinking in work situations or situations that matter is that you may make mistakes. However, you do need people to be able to think of you – not as a know it all – but as someone who is honest and can be trusted by others.

Never be afraid of being judged for what you think or the thing you say, because living in fear of being judged is worse. The truth is that people often respect those who are unafraid to be themselves; don't apologize for who you are. Be yourself freely and express yourself without remorse – you will see that your social life improves drastically, simply because people are so taken by your openness and honesty and pride in your sense of self. And you know that the only way to do this would be making sure you understand your own emotions and know what you want.

## Make New Friends

When you master your emotions and you understand the emotional level and state of other people, it becomes easier for you to make new friends. When the people around you see how emotionally improved you are and they will naturally feel comfortable around you. Making new friends means expanding your social circle; this means that you will have more people who support you. You have more social connections that will help you when you are in need of something. And this will increase your confidence and help you achieve your goals in life.

You will find that mixing with all kinds of people opens up your emotional intelligence to all kinds of possibilities because there will be all different types of people and circumstances. If you have so far struggled between your work and home life, you need to have distinct areas and make the most of both your work situation and your home situation. All too often people live in their work, and give little time to friends and family and this can make your emotional intelligence stifled because you are not open to listening to the needs of people who depend upon you. You must have met people who are so wrapped up in their work that it's hard to talk about other things, or people who are so wrapped up in their social lives that they talk about nothing else even if they are in the workplace. Both sides of the coin are negative because people with emotional intelligence are able to adjust their approach to the environment that they are in. They will know the needs of family members and meet them as well as being responsible enough to understand the necessity to work without the interruption of introducing too much personal information.

If you are short on friends, try to socialize more. Shy people often find comfort in joining classes for things that they are interested in because this brings them closer to people with like interests. You may even find that you want to improve your health and flexibility and joining a gym or even taking up yoga classes can get you to meet others who are like minded. It's a good idea to be kind to people of all ages. Emotionally intelligent people won't dismiss old folk as being a waste of space. Instead, they will understand the difficulties faced by them and be able to help. They will not dismiss the wants and needs of children either and will be able to adjust their emotional approach to kids so that they can empathize with them and make stronger relationships.

## Making Sure You Establish an Understanding

As we have been learning, a huge part of improving your social EQ is understanding and empathizing with the emotions of others around you. Only your high EQ will make your friendships and relationships last longer, since you have established an emotional understanding with that person. Therefore, it is important that people with low EQ must work hard on improving their emotional intelligence, so that there will not be any communication problems and they will be able to make their relationships last longer. If you come across people who have a low emotional intelligence, don't dismiss them. Try to show by example what communication does and how their moods affect the amount of work that they do. This extra insight will help to make them more effective in their lives and that's got to be good either from a personal or from a work point of view.

## Maintaining Current Relationships

People say that nobody stays in your life forever. Though not entirely false, you can make the friendships and relationships in your life last longer by improving your EQ. Maintain your relationships is not only good for your social life but also your personal improvement. As we said above, the more people you have in your life the better, but I would also state that the more solid relationships you have in your life, the more you are able to increase your emotional intelligence because you are surrounded by people who trust you and who accept you for who you are and that's important for your own sense of self or sense of self-esteem.

You might think that people change over time, which is true because everyone is subjected to change. But just as the people around you change, you must also learn to adapt and change for the better. And this can be done by improving your EQ. This way, you can maintain your relationship with other people longer and establish stronger bonds with them. However, you also remember that if a tie does get broken, you should not be dejected and give in to irrational thoughts. You must keep thinking positive and keep moving on. In fact, if you analyze why relationships end, perhaps you can rekindle them by making more effort. These may be people who have moved out of your area but who you hold in high regard. Even if it's your fault that you didn't keep in touch, a phone call goes a long way to repairing the damage and keeping these valuable people as friends.

These are the basic thing you need to focus on while trying to improve your EQ in your social life. Your emotional intelligence isn't counted by the number of "friends" you have on your Facebook page or how many followers you have on "Twitter." Foster relationships in your real life and make sure that your online life leaves room for plenty of social interaction of a real kind. If you are in the company of people, put your cell phone away because constantly looking at it can destroy your emotional intelligence simply because you may not be taking much notice of what is actually happening in your life. People are quickly losing touch with what is important by putting such reliance upon their Internet connection or by playing with their cell phones. If you are going to use it, use it to some productive purpose. For example, it may be a good way of keeping notes about what you learned about people or indeed what you managed to learn about yourself during the course of a particularly emotional day.

Now close your eyes for a moment. Imagine the best friendship that you ever had. Visualize it and see how it developed. Remember events in your life that gave you such a great deal of happiness with those friends. You need to foster more events in your life which matter as much to you and to the participants in those events because these are all food for you to feed on when you are trying to improve your emotional intelligence. They are opportunities for you to learn and to grow as a human being and when you see the value of people that you surround yourself with, you are better able to read them, to empathize and to understand their emotional processes and how this translates into actions or deeds.

# CHAPTER SEVEN

# EMOTIONAL INTELLIGENCE AT YOUR WORK PLACE

You learned how to use your EQ in your social life. Now in this chapter, you will learn how to use it in your office or work place. We have already hinted in a couple of the chapters that led to this one of ways that you can use emotional intelligence to spur people on to working more efficiently, but we will explain this in more detail within the pages of this chapter.

## Make Sure You Understand Yourself

First of all, make sure that you understand your own emotions. Try observing how your emotions and your behavior are connected. When you feel a strong emotion, notice how you react.

To put it simply, when you are faced with a situation, instead of reacting, take a step back and examine what you are feeling in that moment. Look at the instinctive response that is on the tip of your tongue – what emotion is it? Why are you feeling it? What triggered this response? The more and more you understand what triggers your specific behavioral impulses, the better your EQ becomes. And once you know what your behavioral pattern is, you can navigate and manage it better in the future. Take diary notes if you think that this will help. There are several emotional responses that may make you work harder, but you also need to be aware of those that will hinder your work because these emotions may be ones that are holding you back in your career.

Here are a few instances of different types of behaviors and the meaning behind them:

• While feeling embarrassed or insecure, you might withdraw from conversation with others and disconnect. This can be very embarrassing in a work situation because you need better people skills especially when you meet new people and are faced with different scenarios in your everyday work.

- When you are angry, you may end up raising your voice and speaking at a loud volume or even yelling; you could also march away in anger or have the urge to physically harm someone. You do need to manage your anger and if you have emotional intelligence will know that anger fuels negativity. Some people use anger to distance themselves from a situation that made them feel uncomfortable and actually achieve more physical work. If this is the case with you, it's better to do something physical that helps you to calm down, rather than spoil a relationship with a colleague that you count on in your everyday work life.

- When you feel overwhelmed or panicky, it is possible that you will not be able to focus on what you are doing. You will probably lose track of whatever you were doing and start crying, or even have a panic attack. In a situation such as this, learn to use what we have told you about breathing to get back to your normal state where you are no longer panicking. If you take action while you are feeling emotions such as this, you are likely to make mistakes that you may regret. It is better to step away, do a few breathing exercises and then face whatever it is that you need to face.

## Make sure that you adapt yourself

Once you understand your emotions, you can start learning to adapt yourself to your office or your work place environment. Since you are improving at understanding other people, find colleagues with a similar mindset to you. This should not be too hard because their mind is similar yours and you can easily understand their emotions. Working with these people will help you to adapt easily and it will also increase the total output of your group.

If you want your emotional intelligence to grow, make sure that you understand other people's emotions and that includes people that are not of the same mindset as you. Make a note of their emotion and how it affected their workload. You may find that their workload varies depending upon their state of mind. That's normal but once you are able to read people, you can judge who would make great team leaders and motivate others and which employees are the best to work independently and be trusted to do jobs that you delegate to them. If you have a team with all strong leaders, sometimes egos can get in the way of actual work being achieved, so it's important to understand the mindset of different groups of people.

In one office scenario, a change of the layout of the office completely changed the dynamics of the office and the amount of work that got done. You may ask what this has to do with emotional intelligence but it actually had a lot to do with it. Because certain members of staff were uncomfortable with other members of staff, by changing the layout so that their contact with those negative influences was less, the staff were able to do more work.

## Show Empathy

Even though we have covered this in our social life skills, I am talking about this again because empathy is one quality that everyone around you responds to. Everyone around you wants to be understood including yourself. Since you know how important it is for you to be understood, you must give what you want from others in order to get back the same. Showing empathy will gain good favor with your colleagues and you will have a lasting bond with them. Your work efficiency will increase and will earn the respect of the people who work around and with you. And it makes your work place a pleasant environment to be in.

While you don't need to know the ins and outs of every staff member's personal life, knowing a little about it helps you considerably. For example, you will get to know who has the need to work longer hours and why and what kind of work they excel in. That way, you get the best of both worlds by offering them what they need, but on your own terms.

Knowing that you have people working for you who work better when they are pressured, you are able to add the pressure that they need, whilst other members of staff may drop in productivity if they are given too much to do. In that case, you need to work out how their emotions work so that you can use those emotionally fruitful times to ask for more work to be done. Everyone has moments when they are more receptive than others and knowing their emotional needs is helpful to you because you can respond in a way that maximizes the productivity of the workplace.

## Make Sure You Listen

Don't you just hate that feeling when you are talking and you suddenly notice that the person you are talking stopped listening to you or never was in the first place?! Judging by own reaction, you should realize by now that listening to your colleague or other people at your work place is very important. People pay attention to you when you listen to them. They form a good opinion of you when they notice that you are a good listener. And they also tend to trust you more. And when a good trust is built, it becomes easier to work with them and you can achieve your goals more easily. Listening goes further than that. Sometimes, people are so keen to give out information that they interrupt the flow of conversation by changing the subject. This is a really bad thing to do and if you find yourself doing it, try to stop yourself in your tracks. What this does is show that you have a total disregard for the person that you are talking to and can alienate people and make them feel that you don't have time to listen to what they have to say.

This is particularly relevant in the work environment. By listening to people, you get to know which members of staff have ideas that are a potential to improve productivity, but you will never know unless you take the time to listen. Similarly, at meetings, make sure that everyone gets their time to speak because even in the smallest of ideas lies genius and you won't recognize it if you are not listening attentively.

Listening also helps your personal relationships. When your wife or husband is upset about something, listening helps to calm the situation, but it does more than that. It keeps you informed about what that person is feeling and why, so you can use your emotional intelligence to make things right. In one case related to me by a marriage counselor, a man was totally shocked when his wife left him, although everyone saw it coming except him. He was so out of touch with the way that his partner was feeling because he always spoke and expected to be listened to but never took the time to listen, showing a very low level of emotional intelligence.

## Analyze and Anticipate

Keep a close eye on the environment you inhabit, the people around you and the situations you face in day to day life. Analyze your responses to these external stimuli and try to understand yourself in relation to these. Anticipate what the people or person working with you or around you might say. Try to anticipate their emotions and be ready to act or respond accordingly. This does not have to work or be right all the time. It is good to anticipate, so that the communication and bond between your colleagues will improve. And once again it will lead to an increase in your efficiency and output. The more practice you have, the more accurate your hunches will be and your emotional intelligence will increase as a direct result of actually taking note of what is happening and how people react to your responses.

# Be Accepting of the Differences

When you do find a group of people with a mindset similar to yours, you can still never expect two people to have the exact same emotional configuration. There will always be differences in one way or another. So you must always have an open mind about the opinions and mind set of the people around you. Learning to accept differences as part of your life, adapting to the changes and letting people live as they would want to is every bit as important as being able to express your own self freely. You must understand that they will have a different reaction from that of yours to various situations. In those circumstances you must try to be understanding and accepting. This way your colleagues will learn to accept the differences they see in you because you do the same for them.

The good thing about accepting the differences is that you are acknowledging that others have a different mindset and are emotionally intelligent enough to know that this does not make their ideas any less valid than yours. That's a great way to be if you are in business because you will come across people from all walks of life but still be able to gain the same level of respect.

## Be a team

Differences in colleagues need not always be bad. You can efficiently make use of these differences and learn to be more productive as a team. It is like the different curve of each member of the team come together to complete a perfect circle. This will improve the communication between each members of the team and your efficiency as a whole.

Some of these ways may not apply to you if you are a team leader or an employer. There are ways to make sure that you create a good working environment for the people working under you. I have detailed some of these values below so that you can see clearly what you need to do to improve the situation within the workplace. As a leader, you need to follow the advice given below:

## Develop Your Listening Skills

When it comes to developing communication skills, learning to listen and comprehend does not always get the respect and importance these skills deserve. Listening skills perform a dual function; not only do you learn to understand what another person is saying, you also learn to figure out what they are not saying and the significance of those unspoken ideas. Hidden meanings and messages always exist; to understand the subtext, you have to listen carefully to the original message without faltering attention. This is particularly important to you, as a leader, because those hidden messages may lead you in a different direction from that direction you originally intended, but it may be a direction that is more productive and that wins you more respect.

In a day-to-day situation, when you 'listen', you are not actually paying close attention; your brain is more involved with responding to what you've perceived rather than actually paying attention.

Here is a fun technique to develop your listening skills. Find yourself a partner and the two of you sit together. Get one person to speak on a topic for a couple of minutes; it can be about anything and the other person should not know what you're going to speak about before you start. The other person is also not allowed to talk during this time. And at the end, the other person should repeat back to the speaker what they said, or what they thought they heard.

## Show a Genuine Interest in the People You Lead

When you are a leader who possesses a high amount of emotional intelligence, you will find that you are respected and followed without question. This is because such a leader will take the time to get to know their team members; not only will you ask for their names, you will also try to get to know them as actual people instead of just a number in your dossier. You will learn about their interests, hobbies, passions, etc. And when you show a genuine interest in their lives, take them to be people instead of just a categorical 'workforce', they will feel valued and want to live up to what they perceive to be your expectation. In short, they will develop a sense of loyalty to you that will not exist if they are simply 'paid to work'

Let me give you an example. A manager of a company kept for himself a small file, wherein he wrote down all the details of the people in his staff. Obviously, you cannot keep every birthday, every wedding day and the like straight in your mind; his notes allowed him to remember these things and he would often arrange for small gifts, like greeting cards to be sent to them on those days. For a conversation with them, he would consult the file beforehand to make sure to converse with them about topics of their interest. His employees were often amazed at how he could remember so much about the large number of staff under him despite his busy work load.

Doing small things like this will create a big impact on the minds of your employees. And it will improve the communication between you.

## Delegate

In any business, it goes without saying that you need to uphold your own brand vision. However, a lot of leaders have this attitude of nobody-can-do-better-than-I-can. To make your business reach new heights, you will need to trust your team with the brand vision you have created. When you allow them to work as much for the vision as you yourself do, it will show in their work. Delegating is a sign of strength, not weakness – it shows that you are confident in your training of your employees to let them complete the task you've set. It is also necessary from a physical perspective; you're only one person. The less you delegate, the more you have to do yourself. The more the work that piles up, the less productive you are going to end up being.

Now delegating is not to be done lightly; these are tasks that have to be done to precision and you need to pick the right kind of people to do the right kind of jobs. This is where EQ comes into play. A good leader may not be experienced or have all the required knowledge, but he will be able to identify who is suited to what task and will not hesitate to assign it to them. This is where getting to know your employees makes a huge difference; find out what your team's strengths are and capitalize on them. Identify who likes doing what; the more they enjoy their work, the better they will perform. When you delegate to your team, they understand they you trust them and they will want to do their best to not let you down. It will also free time for you to work on those tasks that cannot or should not be delegated and improve the overall efficiency of the company.

## Have Confidence

There will be times when your company is not working as it should be or your brand vision is just that – a vision. When something like this happens, the most important thing for you – as a leader – is not to panic. Your team is going to be looking to you to guide them – you need to remain calm and stoic so as to help boost their team morale. The idea is to remain confident and reassure your team members that failures and setbacks are commonplace and that they need to work hard to overcome them instead of panicking and running away. Keep in mind that they way you react is what your team will react to as well – see how EQ plays a role here? Your staff take their cues from you, so be calm, be confident and be energetic in the face of eminent threat. At the same time, relate to their emotions and be an understanding and supportive leader.

## Have a Positive Attitude

Another aspect of EQ is understanding that your employees are not robots and require down time too. Even within the space of the office, you need to allow them to unwind and have fun. Your own positive and sunny attitude will help a big deal – the more energetic and fun you make out your behavior to be, the more they will also behave the same way.

Also do small things like providing snacks, coffee, maybe even a drink occasionally, etc. Make your employees your friends and get to them as people instead of staff members; exchange relationship advice, recipes and whatever else that could make them feel like they belong. Keep the environment at the workspace balanced between playfulness and productivity. Not only will you earn their trust and loyalty, you will also see their efficiency improve. And your own attitude towards your work becomes more positive too!

## Show Commitment

Being an emotionally intelligent leader means leading by example. You may not be brilliant at the nitty-gritty details of business; that's what you hire your staff for. As a leader, you are required to do hard work, understand your employees and help them perform better. Your team will respect you only when you are willing to show the brand vision the same amount of commitment you expect from them. It will also instill within them the need to work as hard as you and you will see the efficiency and productivity of your team rise up.

Once you have gained the respect of your team, they will probably deliver the peak amount of quality work possible. And you will also be satisfied emotionally, because the environment you have created for yourself is stress free and you can still keep working on increasing your EQ.

So by flowing these steps, you can really improve your EQ at your work place, be more efficient and get closer to achieving your goals.

As you can see from all of these skills listed above, you are in a very complex situation but the more emotional intelligence you employ during the course of your working life, the more success you will reap. People respond well to those leaders who know how much emotional intelligence comes into play when dealing with people. They respect you because they know that you are looking at things from a very fair standpoint, as opposed to the team leader who can only see things in the way he intended without making any adjustment for different mindsets, bending circumstances of any of the other things that can get in the way of efficiency within the workplace and particularly within the team. There are always going to be weak links within a team but a leader who has emotional intelligence will be able to put those weak links into jobs that will help them to feel self-satisfaction and drive to do well so that their inability to match the skills of other members will still fall into the category of being efficient.

# CHAPTER EIGHT

# HOW TO IMPROVE YOUR EMOTIONAL INTELLIGENCE IN YOUR GENERAL LIFESTYLE

EQ is not a concept that is completely abstract; it can be learnt and developed in very realistic ways. We learnt how to use EQ in our social lives and our work place. In this chapter we are going to elaborately learn how to improve our emotional intelligence in your day to day approach to life. First, I will tell you how to start small by using these following strategies:

• Keep an eye on how you react to other people. See if you rush to judgment before you know all of the facts. Be honest with yourself – identify each interaction with each person and how they differ from one another. Now try putting yourself in their shoes; when you do that, you will instinctively be open to their perspectives and emotional needs. This is a particularly good exercise to try with your spouse and with your children because parents make some terrible mistakes along the way by not feeling empathy toward their children. They assume because they are older and are the parents that they are always right, when in fact this is often not the case. Listen to your children and learn to know them better as human beings and learn also that one standard answer doesn't fit all. You need to experience empathy to be able to understand which tactics work best with which child.

• Observe your work environment. Notice if you seek attention for the accomplishments you have achieved. Humility is wonderful quality, and do not think that it means that you're shy or that you lack self-confidence. Don't be so bothered about receiving praise; let your co-workers shine too and let them attain the spotlight – it won't make you any less valued as an employee! The problem here is that people who do seek attention for the good things that they do need to work on their self-esteem as much as anything else. It's actually very irritating to have a member of staff who is always looking for validation. Make that validation the fact that you were trusted to do the job, rather than always seeking out spoken validation just because a lacking self-esteem needs it. If you can do this, you are more likely to be trusted with more serious jobs and senior positions because you are not showing yourself to be emotionally needy.

• Do a self-evaluation. Assess your weaknesses. Remember, you are not perfect – no human being is. Unless you accept this simple fact, you will not be able to make a change for the better. Have the courage to analyze and criticize yourself honestly. This goes for all kinds of activities during the day. Stop and think:

o Why did I react in that way?

o How could I have handled it in a better way

o Why am I failing to grasp the severity of a situation

o What are the emotions that are driving me

o        Do I need to adjust my emotions to be better suited to the task

o        Why am I getting so upset about this?

o        What caused the upset and what is the root case?

o        What are the emotions that are attached to this situation?

o        How can I overcome the negative impact of my emotions in this situation?

That might look like an awful lot of evaluation but when you are trying to improve your emotional intelligence, you improve it by learning about your responses, your emotional triggers and what causes them and this puts you in better control of situations and of your life in general.

•        Notice your reactions to stressful situations. See if you become upset every time there's a delay or if things don't turn out the way you planned. Another thing to keep an eye out for is whom you put the blame on for mistakes – putting too much on yourself is not good. Neither is unduly blaming another person even when they haven't done anything. You also have to realize that staying calm and in control of any difficult situation is essential. Make sure to keep your emotions under control when things go south.

- Learn to <u>take responsibility</u> for all your actions. <u>Apologize</u> directly if you had hurt someone's feelings – that means that you cannot simply avoid the person you wronged or pretend the situation didn't happen! Own up to your issues – if you make an honest attempt to make things right you will find that people won't have too much difficulty forgiving you and moving on with their lives. In all honesty, nobody has the time or the energy to hold a long grudge in this fast paced world. Apologizing for something that you did wrong isn't that hard and it changes a situation entirely.

o People stop feeling angry because someone took responsibility

o People stop harboring grudges because they feel for your mistake o      You begin to learn from the mistake that you made

o      You acknowledge weakness which endears other to you

- Before you take an action, always make sure that you examine how your actions will affect others. Think about how the other person would feel if you went ahead and did this. Or examine whether you yourself would want such an experience. If you decide that this action absolutely must be taken, then also examine the possible ramifications and how you can mitigate any trouble caused to other people.

Now that you have learned the basics of how to start improving your emotional intelligence, I will elaborate on the various ways you can improve your EQ.

The best way to improve any emotional intelligence is to practice it in real life. When you do it daily and you also try to get feedback on any changed behaviors you display, you will be able to gauge your own EQ. You will become more efficient in identifying and managing your own emotions and that of others.

All of us have an aspect of our lives that we can improve. Here is a list of things you can do to improve your EQ. Each skill has its own merit and will help your overall EQ, but you may find that one skill is particularly more helpful than the others in a specific type of situation.

## Examine your emotional reactions to events all through the day:

It is very easy to maintain a notebook in which you write down all the feelings you experienced during the course of the day. But that is not enough – you need to make an honest attempt to acknowledge those feelings and validate them. Each experience will trigger a particular response and emotion within you – ignoring your feelings means that you are not taking into account information that shapes the way you think and the way your mind works, which in turn, influence the way you behave. So from now on, start paying more attention to your feelings and when you do, connect them to specific experiences.

For instance, let us say that you are cut off from speaking or completing your presentation during a professional meeting. Examine how you feel at this. Most of us would feel embarrassed, angry or irritated, but rarely do we allow ourselves to process the emotion or label it as such. We end up ruminating on the emotion without examining it closely and in the end, feel only resentful or bitter and don't really move on. Identify every emotion you feel and don't disown anything. Start tapping into your emotions at certain times every day. Also, in your notebook, make a note of the first emotion you wake up to and the last emotion you feel before you fall asleep.

## Do not judge your own emotions:

Even if you're emotions are negative, they are all valid. We have a habit of invalidating negative feelings by constantly reinforcing this belief that positivity is the way to go. I am not saying that it isn't, just that you need to let yourself feel those negative emotions if you want to purge yourself of them.

When you become judgmental of your own emotions, you inhibit your ability to feel them and deal with them in a positive manner. Each feeling you experience is information that is tied in to a particular thing that's happening in your world. You will not know how to adequately react if you do not know that information. This is the reason why being able to feel and understand your emotions is called 'intelligence'.

It will initially be hard, but you must start practicing allow yourself to feel the negative emotions as much as the positive ones. You must connect them to what's happening around you. At the same time, learn to fully experience your positive emotions. When you know what makes you happy or sad, you can pick out ways to be happier and avoid the situations that make you sad.

## Practice deciding how to behave:

Remember – you cannot control what you feel. Emotions are irrational; you have no actual control over them. What you can control is how you respond to them and how to express them. If you have an anger management issue like lashing out or if you shut down when you're hurt, reconsider another alternative from the way you usually react. Identify the way you react, identify whether it's positive or negative and then see what you can do to ensure that your emotions do not overwhelm you.

If something negative or unpleasant happens to you, stop there and analyze what your emotions are at that time. The situation might make you angry or sad. Don't run from that sadness – allow yourself to feel it in full. When that first initial wave passes, identify how you would like to react. You could sit and wallow or you could move and do something about it. You could also talk to someone to help alleviate the burden on your shoulder. Communicating your feelings instead of repressing them will help you even more.

Do not try to escape from it or try to suppress it by drinking too much, or watching television or reading too much to numb whatever sadness you're feeling. Doing this often will only affect your EQ in a bad way.

## Become more self-aware:

Self-awareness is one of the vital areas of emotional intelligence. It somewhat acts as the cornerstone of all the other areas of EQ. You must know your own feelings first if you are to understand and respond to the feelings of the people in your life. Being self-aware doesn't come easy – you could try meditating or doing simple reflection exercises to identify your own emotional state. Exercises like yoga and mediation will allow you to be aware of both your body and your mind, thereby letting you learn to control your response to stimulus.

Increase your emotional vocabulary by noting down your emotions at various situations along with time intervals in a notebook. Write down what you feel at each instance in this notebook – this will let you identify patterns and processes to your emotions that will help you improve your EQ and behavior.

Start rating your emotions on a scale of 1 to 10. It becomes easier to keep track of your emotions this and change your behavior if necessary.

It becomes easier to manage your emotions if you know how to express them freely. Most people do not share what they truly feel with anyone else for fear of being judged. But this approach is a lot harder than you think and it will make your life very lonely. Man is a social animal, and whether you want to admit it or not, we need to form intimate and personal relationships with others. Don't let yourself be lonely by not being open and honest about what you feel. You don't need to have 1000 Facebook friends – you just need one friend you can lean on unconditionally.

## Discover your true passions:

All of us go about doing our work day after day. But how many of us are really passionate about the work we do? Many of us feel that we are stuck in a rut at our jobs. But we must understand that we did not just magically jump into our jobs. We end up where we are by following either the opportunities that were given to us or by money or through the people we know and end up in our current job.

Only a handful of people actually attempt to get into the field of work that they are passionate about. Each and every one of us has our own passion, buried deep within us. We might not always find it easy to explore them. Chances are you will probably know some starving artists who have given up their daily jobs so that they can struggle to achieve their dreams. Finding work that you're passionate about might not be that easy, but it will make your life meaningful and give you purpose. Otherwise you'll just wonder at the monotony of your days and give up.

## Determine your strength and weakness:

Understanding yourself will help you make the right choices in life. If you focus on your strengths, you will get more from life.

When you do those things that you are passionate about (at which you will instinctively be good at), you will be able to live a richer and fuller life. Do not keep worrying about those areas you are weak at, unless they interfere with your life. You are only holding yourself back from getting the most out of life.

The idea of choosing what to do based on 'your gut' is a euphemism for using your EQ to make choices. While some choices will feel good, other choices might give you an uneasy feeling. Your gut is just your emotional intelligence guiding you, even if you don't consciously acknowledge it. This means that you need to be well aware of strengths and weaknesses; you cannot make half-cocked decisions based on faulty information.

## Walk in the other person's shoes:

One of the most powerful emotions is empathy. The most successful leaders, politicians, philanthropists and star personalities became so successful only because of their inherent empathy.

You can get closer to the people around you if you learn how to empathize with them. And when you do that, you will win their support when you need it, which may help you defuse a potentially high-charged situation. If you can prove to someone that you know where they are coming from, that you truly understand their hardships and want to help them, you will earn both their respect and loyalty. It will show them that you are not self-centered and that you acknowledge the feeling of others around you.

Observe the people you spend your day with; it will help you increase your empathy toward them. While communicating with another person, listen very carefully. Make sure you pay close enough attention that you comprehend both what they want to say and what they want you to hear. You become more empathic by listening to what they say; pick up on the things that affect them and act accordingly.

When you can learn empathy, this opens up a whole lot of opportunity because you see things not only from your own point of view but from the point of view of the person with whom you are dealing. That makes your part in the whole picture more powerful. You are able to feel their emotions. You can also see quite logically how their emotions affect whatever is being discussed and will be able to adjust situations to make them a lot better for all concerned.

We take one step ahead of empathy in the next chapter and show you how to read the mood of people you are dealing with and use that to help you to succeed. This is empathy, but it's empathy put to good use. When you learn to handle people, regardless of their emotional state, you also learn a lot about real management. You are able to find a balance so that you can find solutions that work for everyone. People with a high level of emotional intelligence and stability are able to find solutions where perhaps there were not many solutions to be had. If you look at the great leaders of our times in working with the poor, these are people who used emotional intelligence to be able to calm the storms of life.

Remember, panic is not an option. Calm listening skills and picking up on the mood of others can help you to make a better approach to them and get results. If you offer a starving child a roof over his head, it isn't addressing his emotional need. If you offer him a crust of bread so that he can feel better than starving in that moment in time, then you will have used your emotional intelligence and will have won his allegiance and that's vital.

Similarly with children, if you want to lead the kids, don't try to be one. You are not one. Your emotional intelligence may assist you in showing your kids that you know how to have fun but you cannot pretend that you are a child because there will always be that difference between you and the children. Pick up on what they are thinking and work a way around those thoughts and emotions to really get close to your kids as leader of the pack because when you do, you win an allegiance that is virtually indestructible.

# CHAPTER NINE

# TRY MANAGING ANOTHER PERSON'S EMOTIONS

Being able to manage emotions of another person is quite the impressive skill to have. The leaders who possess this ability are the leaders who can calm or reassure an agitated crowd and then control them. And then, there are those who mismanage the emotions of the people around them. The leaders whose body language is shifty, who dodge questions and give non-answers, who use evasion as a technique to control audience just get tomatoes thrown at their faces – they don't comprehend the emotions of the people watching them and don't know how to play on those feelings.

Being able to manage another's emotions is not as hard as it sounds. Just follow these steps –

## Increase your empathy

We have already covered this. So simply put, you have to imagine yourself in the other's position and try to identify what you might feel in such a situation.  You can learn to better empathize with them by speaking to them and observing their reactions closely during times of crises. Find out if they like sports, exercise or what their favourite meal is, the teams they support and the activities that they like. Get to know the person so that you can feel more empathy towards them – obviously, a stranger's problem is hardly going to make an impact on you although, when you have a great deal of emotional intelligence it can. Let me give you an example of how I used the emotions of someone else to gain something from them. In one office where I worked, there was an employee who would never do her share of work when she was miserable. Instead of doing that, she would sit and moan for much of the day and people would half listen to her problems and then go on with whatever they had to do. Because no one really listened to her and everyone saw her as a miserable woman, they kind of skirted around her all day and the misery could continue all the way through from nine to five.

Being in charge of this particular office, I decided that this wasn't the way to do things. She was looking for validation of some kind of another. I had already seen her in a state when she was angry at one stage and during this anger produced much more work than she usually did. Thus, I pulled her to one side at lunch time and sat down and listened to the complaints that she had in her life. I didn't know her very well at all but she related all of her misery and I empathized. At the end of listening to what she had to say – and believe me it was difficult to keep a straight face at times – I actually showed her how good she was at her job and said that instead of being upset and letting it all get to her – she should be angry and that in her place, I certainly would be.

The trick worked. She transferred her emotions from feeling pathetic and doing nothing to feeling like she could conquer the world and being very productive indeed. In fact, even people around her noticed the difference in her attitude and were the first to congratulate her when she achieved as much as she did. This helped to boost her moral and by the time she left the office that day, she felt happy and content inside instead of miserable and making it last several days. The empathy that I was able to show toward her took effort, but it was worthwhile because we both won out at the end of the day and quotas were met without difficulty.

Not everyone will respond in this way, but by observing the emotions of others over a period of time, you can pretty well gage what mood will produce what amount of work. You can also gage how much a person is likely to do if they are taken away from the source of their emotional problem. If coworkers are making each other's lives miserable, splitting them up and placing them in separate areas solves several problems and makes the productive hours that they spend at work more worthwhile.

## Respond to someone the way you would expect others to respond to you in times of pain

Helping another person manage their emotions is easier said than done; you need to first identify what you want them to feel and then figure out how you are supposed to get them there. You must also remember that you can't force someone to feel something – you can only help them come to terms with what they're already feeling or to move in a more positive direction.

For an inspirational speaker or for a movie that is supposed to move people, it needs an impactful experience or story. An impactful experience usually involves a build-up in which the speaker or movie director sets the stage or situation for where they want to take you emotionally. You have to try to create this kind of an environment for the person you're communicating with so that they go where you want them to go.

Obviously, you need to reassure them that you're firmly on their side. Tell them about a similar experience you had just like theirs but make it real. When your message is consistent with your tone of voice or your body language, it will help them see that you're only trying to help and they will be able to come to terms with any negative feelings they are having. Don't make up things that they will see as being false because if they do see that you are just trying to get them out of their negative emotional state – no matter what it takes – they will lose respect for you.

# Improve your non-verbal communication:

Being able to communicate well does not mean that you need to have just verbal skills and the ability to manage stress. More often than not, it's how you say what you're saying that makes more difference than what you're saying itself. The non-verbal cues that others pick up on, like your hand gestures, your posture, the pace of your speech, the volume of your voice, the eye contact you make, etc., are what they will judge you on.

If you want to hold the attention of others and build with them a good rapport, you have to be both aware of and in control of your body. This kind of communication is two-way; you also need to be able to pick up on the non-verbal cues that the others send out and then adjust your own behavior accordingly.

You must understand that these messages are not restricted to the time a person is speaking alone. Even when there is nothing but silence, you are nonverbally communicating with them. These non-verbal cues can be positive or negative; you could interest, excite and make your audience desire more contact with you or you could bore them and confuse or frighten them as well. So make sure that you are understood even if you cannot be heard.

While communicating, you must always focus on the other person. If you are too busy thinking about your own dialogue, you will miss the non-verbal cues and possibly mess up. Make eye contact – it will show that you have interest, it makes the flow of a conversation easy, and it helps gauge the response of the person you are talking to. Also, do not forget to pay attention to nonverbal cues that you send and receive, like your expression, your tone of voice, your posture and your gestures. These will help improve your non-verbal communication.

When you have a handle on the way that people think, you are much better equipped to deal with all of the things that can arise in life. You are more empathetic, but you also learn an important lesson and that's humility. No matter how poor or badly off people may seem, there are always those strong stars that shine through and amaze you. If you stop looking you don't see them. If you continue through your life trying to understand how people tick, it's almost certain that you will. When you do, it makes you feel humble and the best communicators with the highest emotional intelligence will acknowledge that surprises lay in wait all of the time and that not all of them are bad.

# CHAPTER TEN

# LEARN TO BE SOCIALLY RESPONSIBLE

One of the things that will give you high levels of emotional experience is being socially responsible. It will show to others that you really care about them, especially people who are less fortunate. Remember that having socially responsibility not about garnering a better reputation or personal gain – it's giving back to those who are not as fortunate as you have been. This helps you to gain stature but you need to do it just because you know it needs doing, rather than because you want some kind of praise at the end of it. It's not about you. It's about learning the responsibility that comes with being emotionally intelligent.

## Different levels of Social Responsibility

The most basic thing you can do is donate money to charity or a worthy cause. Donations are only a first step in the process. The problem with this kind of giving is that it's often without emotion. It's like paying a bill and although it may be a worthwhile cause, you need to really believe in the cause.

One of the best that I have found for doing this is an organization called Kiva who help people to get back onto their feet in dire circumstances. You may be helping out with a twenty five dollar loan so that a village in Africa can add a water filter to their village pump. You may be loaning an Ethiopian mother twenty five dollars because she wants to buy a sewing machine. What you are doing when you invest in loans such as this is show your emotional intelligence. You are helping those who are prepared to get up and help themselves though the only thing standing in their way is lack of money. You help to make people more self-sufficient and are not giving money away to charities where you don't know where the pennies are going. It gives you a great conversation piece to try and gain more interest from others and you get your money back. In this case, you can then go on to help someone else. So instead of a one off payment to society and thinking that is enough, you are kept ever conscious of the needs of the world and as one twenty five dollars comes back to you are able to make this a rolling event so that you are always contributing and that's far more intelligent.

Help a worthy organization collect money for their cause. You can ask for donations from your friends, your family, or from people at your work place. It will also help if you get involved in events that raise money. One of the most recent things that people are getting involved in is raising money for cancer research. You don't have to look far to find people who have been affected by cancer within their family. These are the kind of people who can sponsor you to walk or sponsor you to climb a mountain because they learn that what this money is being used for is to improve the lot of human beings who may face cancer in the future. You will always gain support, but along the way, you become more emotionally intelligent because some of the people you meet are so amazing.

Social responsibility will be more effective if you involve yourself personally by giving to a good cause that can help improve people's lives. Start by identifying those social issues you're most passionate about; if you don't feel passionate about a social cause, you're less likely to want to make a contribution and you are less likely to gain anything emotional from it.

Once you have picked out a cause that you want to support, start thinking of the best ways to contribute to it. Either you can volunteer yourself or you could support via monetary donations. Go to the next level by contacting the agency or organization that is paving a way a way that cause and ask how you can make a difference as a single individual.

You may wonder what this has to do with emotional intelligence, but it has rather a lot to do with it because the wider the groups of people that you have something to do with, the more you learn about the way that people live and the more capable you are of exercising humility.

Social responsibility also means that you should watch the way that you connect with others on social networks. You can use emotional intelligence online as well as offline and if you do, your relationships are likely to be positive and not have a negative impact on strangers. Although people do not realize the impact of bad behavior online, it has caused others much emotional distress. Don't be the one to make comments without thought. Just as you would think about what you say offline, use the same courtesy toward others.

Help people in your community if you get a chance because this will also mean that you are giving something back to society and that helps you to feel more viable as a human being. When people have the problem of self-esteem issues, volunteerism is one of the most effective ways of building up the self-esteem providing that all that you do is done for the right reasons. Don't do it for any kind of recognition or reward. Do it because it's your nature and the reward that you get back from it is much longer lasting than expecting people to thank you.

Your social responsibility pattern helps you to see how you are affected by different types of people. It also helps you to open up your levels of understanding which will help you in the workplace because you will have a higher level of emotional intelligence. Fostering this and maturing it by listening and learning is the road toward improving your level of emotional intelligence. If you are going to be online at any time, why not test your emotional intelligence level because your results will help you to see where you are going wrong. There is a test at this link and it's fun and interesting.

# Learn to manage your own impulses in response to others

We already talked about managing your own emotions, and you must realize that it just as important to manage the impulses that your emotions lead to. Here are three ways you can try to manage your impulses as far as responding to the emotions of other people. It is vital if you want to learn sociability and in taking note of these tips, you will find that your emotional intelligence increases.

Distraction - Distracting yourself is easy, so when you feel you are having a problem controlling your emotional impulses at any given moment; distract yourself. This does not mean you drift off from the conversation or situation; you can do things like counting from one to ten or take deep breaths. Training yourself to quickly change your thoughts or the subject in a conversation by talking about the weather or any other event will help you curb your impulses and keep them in control. This is particularly useful for people who do tend to feel impulses that negatively affect the person to whom they are speaking.

Analytic - it means that you must stop yourself and analyze your thoughts when you begin to feel impulsive. Examine your situation and find out why you are reacting that way and see if there is another alternative. If you find that you don't have time to analyze your impulse, make a quick note so that you will remember to look into it at a later time when you can concentrate on it. This is very valuable feedback and helps you to grow as a human being.

Coping: Once you learn to distract and analyze yourself in an effective way, you must learn to cope with it. In order to have a good coping strategy, you must prepare some thoughts in advance. You must think that you can always control your thoughts and believe in that. You must remember that you can always slow down a bit. Think this through and don't rush with your response. And always remember to think of an alternative.

These are good methods by which you will learn to control your impulses. But these will not be effective immediately. By planning them and practicing, you can easily learn to control impulsive thoughts, words, and actions.

# Increase your flexibility:

All of us have a routine way of doing things. There are rules we follow to make sure things run smoothly and efficiently. Unfortunately, more often than not, these rules become set in stone instead of being simple guidelines to help execute our tasks in a timely fashion. Flexibility is the key to success – being too rigid will only cause your opportunities to slip by. You will tend to fall behind in learning new techniques and will tend to solve problems in unproductive ways.

When it's time for change or moving on, people with high EQ will make that adjustment.

If you find change difficult, it's because you are used to where you are right and a change might take you out of your comfort zone. Times like these stop and analyze the possible consequences. Learn to accept that change is part of growth. Being open to changes will help you understand that new experiences and new opportunities will give you a sense of accomplishment and personal satisfaction. Learning new things is difficult no doubt, but it is worth in the long run. Making new relationships, acquiring new skills and the like is what true growth is.

## Use humor deal with the challenges you face:

Life's difficulties can easily be dealt with humor and laughter. Laughter helps you feel lighter and stay calm in the face of adversity. A hearty laugh helps release oxytocin, which will make your mood become positive. It also helps bring your nervous system back into balance.

It becomes easier to take hardships in stride when you learn to communicate playfully. You will be able to look at any disappointments and frustrations you face from a different, more carefree perspective. And it will help you deal better with annoyances and setbacks. It will help smooth over the differences. When you use gentle humor, you will find that it also helps you to express those ideas and feelings that you may not otherwise be able to give voice to.

You will find that you are both relaxed and energized at the same time. Also, it helps you become more creative. The more you let go of your old rigid thinking, the freer your expression becomes and the more you can create.

Start learning embrace your playful and humorous side. Set aside a regular, quality playtime. Things become much easier once you learn to joke about them. Explore activities that you enjoy so that you loosen you up embrace your playful nature. You can start by spending time with animals or children and outgoing people who will appreciate your change and your playful side.

## Learn to be happy:

Stop and honestly see how happy you are. When you posses a high EQ, you will learn to be happier and it will not just be when good things happen to you.

Real happiness comes from the inside out. If you learn to manage your emotions well, you will wake in the morning with a smile on your face. And throughout the day, you will find that you can keep up this level of joy even when you are faced with challenges. The positive mood will help you keep those negative emotions at bay and you will find that your ability to solve problems becomes more pronounced.

When you are happy, you accomplish more. Happiness and sadness do fluctuate, but with high EQ, you will have the ability to control your emotional state such that you can get things done. To be emotionally intelligent means that you know when to be happy, sad, excited or anxious. When you are happy, other people prefer being around you. People will follow you and will be very engaged when you are happy.

Only a few people actually learn how to manage their happiness. Too many people associate happiness with materialistic items. You will find yourself really happy when you actually give more. When you spread happiness around you, you will tend to be happy yourself and it will help you attain a high level of emotional intelligence.

While you develop and improve your emotional intelligence, keep in mind that it costs literally nothing to make someone else smile. And when you try to make others smile, they will do unto you what you do to them, and it becomes a positive cycle of reinforcement and joy that will make you more successful than you've ever been before.

All of the foregoing information depends upon your receptiveness to change. You have to be able to see fault in yourself. You also need to learn that life isn't always walked in a straight line and sometimes your response to changes in the road will show you whether you really do have a heightened level of emotional intelligence. When you come across situations that are out of your control, how do you react? You need to recognize those reactions:

- Some people cry

- Some people are able to adjust

- Some people get angry

- Some get frustrated by the changes

Don't worry if you react in one of these ways to a shocking change in circumstance, but use the knowledge that you gain from observation to help you to adjust the way that you react so that when this kind of event happens again in the future, you are better able to deal with those changes without the frustration, anger or tears.

## Using discussion to discover other people's emotional intelligence

People with a high level of emotional intelligence make the best candidates for debates. If you join a debating society or find a debate site online, you can test your metal against others. It's not a question of arguing. It's a question of persuasion and that's where true emotional intelligence lies. People who have it are able to come up with solutions bearing in mind all the types of people involved in a given scenario.

If you have a local resident's association and are involved in it, this also gives you the opportunity to meet different types of people. Neuro Linguistic programming is all about understanding a wide cross section of cultures because this fosters better results, though if you are able to take a course on this, it will be helpful in its own way but it will also raise your level of awareness of others and mean that you are automatically able to learn to be emotionally intelligent.

Discussions with others give you the opportunity to learn to look at your responses or impulses to any given stimuli and that helps you to see where you may be making mistakes and put them right. If, for example, your response gives you results that you did not anticipate, you need to examine those because this will help you later in life when a similar situation occurs. It may have been your response that triggered the negative reaction and by tweaking the way that you response and taking control of those impulses, you are able to take control of situations that you would not have been capable of controlling before.

When you feel emotional impulses arising, you need to examine them in order to understand your own way of thinking, but don't overthink it. Simply give yourself a little bit of space before you respond so that any negativity that you may have locked up inside you can be examined later, but you don't put a negative emphasis on whatever it is that you are discussing. Negative impulses happen for a specific reason and the examination that you make of self will allow you to see why you respond in such a manner and whether it is justified.

As you can see from this chapter, there is much that you can do to increase your emotional intelligence but also increase your level of understanding of both yourself and you impulses as well as understanding other people. People with emotional intelligence tend to understand that those who do not have this power within their grasp may not respond in the same way that others would. That's the great thing about understanding people. This then allows them to be able to manipulate the situation to the best outcome.

You must remember when you display some kind of negativity that this will affect those around you and it may not be in the most emotionally intelligent way for all kinds of reasons. Your negativity could for example fire up their anger or make them feel that you are not prepared to listen to their reason. It may also increase self-esteem issues in people who are left to feel that their opinions do not count. An emotionally intelligent person knows the difference and doesn't press those triggers because making someone else feel good about themselves will yield better results.

# CHAPTER ELEVEN

# HOW YOUR LIFESTYLE AFFECTS YOUR EMOTIONAL INTELLIGENCE

**W**e have already talked about how emotional intelligence affects people around you or the way that you react to them. Now we want to touch upon how your lifestyle affects your level of emotional intelligence. If you want to maximize the benefits of increasing this, you do need to learn to look after yourself and that's important. We touched on the benefits of relaxation, mindful living and meditation but you should understand that in your everyday life, you need to be kind to yourself. Listening to your body's needs is one way in which you help your levels to rise. If you are not in optimum health because of self-neglect, you are not likely to pick up on the right emotional impulses when you need them. Your mind will be sluggish and your body may feel that its needs are not being met. In the following information, be aware that all of these are necessary as lifestyle changes if you really want to maximize the possibility of becoming more emotionally intelligent.

**Sufficient sleep**

You should always make sure that your body has enough sleep. You cannot be at your optimum levels unless you start the day in the right way. Your subconscious mind needs to have REM or deep sleep so having your regular 8 hours at night is one way that you can optimize the possibility of being able to read people and read your own emotions. If you start the day off tired, you give yourself a decided disadvantage.

**Regular eating of a varied diet**

Your brain needs all the food that allows it to distribute all the vitamins and minerals that your body needs to the different parts of your body for maximum efficiency. Food is fuel. Make sure that you eat the right kind of foods. If you are obese, you need to be able to exercise sufficiently to bring your levels down because any excess weight will be an added disadvantage to you. Eat all the right kinds of foods and make sure that your diet is varied and that you drink plenty of water.

**Exercising your brain**

If you want to increase your emotional intelligence, learn to analyze as this will be a very important tool for critical thinking. This could be incorporated into your home life in your everyday scenarios and to keep the brain sharp, try to ensure that you push yourself beyond your comfortable limits and learn something. Languages are a very useful introduction to your life because these take a lot of analysis and are also opening up your emotions to being expressed in different languages and as other cultures would. This is useful for international business. If you do work abroad, couple your language learning with learning about how people live and how they respond in an emotional way to different stimuli in different cultures. It's very useful work and even if you only find a chance to do this during vacations, it actually makes you think more even when you are communicating in your own language.

**Keeping a journal**

This is an important part of critical thinking but it's also vital to improving your quota of emotional intelligence. If you think that a journal is a little too twee, use an exercise book and use your observations of the reactions you found noteworthy during the course of talking to people. This really will help you to see on the page what you need to change to get better results. You can only improve if you know what you are doing wrong and the more you are able to analyze unusual situations, the better you will understand them and be able to mend any harm done.

Maybe you could have a response section where you give yourself points on the different approaches so that you find which are best for certain circumstances, but be aware that these methods will not always give consistent results. What comes into question is the mentality of the person with whom you are dealing.

## Exercise and fresh air

Everyone needs fresh air and exercise. The trouble with all of this study is that there does come a point when enough is enough and you need to put down your books and take in some fresh air. Know when to stop. Don't overtax your brain with trivial things. The most important emotions that you need to decipher are those that you use in response to given stimuli which surprise you. You may not know yourself as well as you think you do and may be the one who is sabotaging your own chances of success. By keeping a note of things that you observe, you really can improve your life but don't overdo it. When you need to take air, go out for a walk because this helps to clear your head and perhaps you could even follow this walk with a nice relaxation session or a session of meditation.

The way that you live your life will have an impact upon your ability to use emotional intelligence to the max. You don't have to be rich. You don't have to be in the position of being the boss. Emotional intelligence can be used by anyone who is able to put their life into perspective and see things as they really are, rather than ignoring the emotions of people that form part of your life. This means everyone – within your personal and your work life. When you tackle improving your reactions and tackle making yourself happy by living a reasonable lifestyle, you begin to see that it's not money or material success that equates emotional intelligence. You can be as poor as a church mouse, but if you practice critical thinking and emotional intelligence, you will indeed be happier where it counts – because you will be a better person for it.

# CONCLUSION

And now we have reached the end of this book. I honestly hope you found this book useful and I hope that it helped you reach the amount emotional intelligence you wanted to achieve. I pray that you achieve all your goals in life. Keep smiling and have a great life ahead but before we leave you, let's go over some of the things that you need to take from this book into your everyday life. Since you have learned what emotional intelligence is, you need to look at your life in a different way. Instead of blaming others for misunderstandings, look closer at your own approach and see how you could approach similar situations in a more emotionally intelligent way.

We have taught you all about hesitancy, rather than throwing negativity into the mix. We have also discussed writing thoughts and feelings down because by doing this, you are able to learn something from them that you may not otherwise learn. When you examine the way that you reacted to a given situation, you can see quite clearly the patterns that emerge and recognize where your own weaknesses lie. It may be these that stop you from getting promotion. It may even be these that are stopping you from being able to create lasting relationships. Whatever your weakness, this written down information helps you to learn all about yourself.

There are various methods that we have suggested for self-improvement and sufficient slowing down of the mind for you to be able to see life in a clearer way. We have even suggested that you take online emotional intelligence tests to try and see where your weaknesses exist. Within the book, you will find tips about how to communicate in a better way and how to recognize people's emotional issues so that you don't need to trample on others to get what you want. If you can measure their emotional need and meet it when you are negotiating, you are far more likely to gain solid and edifying results.

We would suggest that you keep a note of how you feel every day and mark it perhaps with zero to one hundred scoring, 100 being the highest score. If you find that you are dipping in mood, try and discover why. If you don't have time at the time that you discover this mood standing, then note it in your notebook and let your mind work over it during the course of the day when you have time. If you can work out which moods or emotions fire up the best results, you can tap into that source of extra energy and maximize all of your efforts.

Learn to use active listening. This stills your mind sufficiently to read people in a more effective way. That man who is standing at the door could be someone who is angry or could be someone who is worried. Test yourself on guessing the mood of people and you could even try a game with friends where each of you guesses in turn but you should always be honest with your replies. The more exposure that you have to the different emotions that people feel, the more capable you are of tapping into their emotions to gain the best advantage, no matter what the situation.

We would suggest that you read back through the book and try out some of the exercises that we have suggested. Even if you consider yourself to have a high level of emotional intelligence, there will be areas where you have weaknesses and it is those areas that will need more practice. For example, you may not be that good at reading others, while you may feel that you have all of your own emotions in check. If this is the case, mix with people more and allow yourself the possibility of learning to read others. By using active listening, you get great clues from others about their ability to grasp a certain subject and how they let emotions get in the way.

Lastly, be kind to yourself. In order to maximize the benefits of the emotions that you have in your mind, you need to look after you. That means having enough sleep, eating the right foods and learning to find balance within your life. I have given you basic instructions for meditation and you may wish to push this further. If you do, I would suggest that you take up lessons and would also suggest that you may find it enjoyable to take up Tai Chi or Yoga because both of these disciplines will help you to have a much more fluent mind body connection and that's vital for feeling happy about your life.

There are those who profess to be intelligent. There are those who pretend to be brighter than they are, but the emotionally intelligent will always shine because they base their thoughts not only upon actions but upon how emotions affect actions and you can be sure that this is a serious consideration and something that psychiatrists and scientists believe to be the answer to understanding the human mind and maximizing your own potential to communicate. When you are able to do that, you will be able to take the emotional intelligence test once more and will probably find that your emotional intelligence quota has increased. That's when you will know that the work you put into the effort was worthwhile and you have understood the power of emotional intelligence to enable people to think in a critical manner.

Thanks for reading.

"The only way to change someone's mind is to connect with them from the heart."

**— Rasheed Ogunlaru**

If you can remember that, then the chances are that you have already found out the value of emotional intelligence because it draws the string that allows people to connect to one another in a positive and productive way.

**Free Bonus Guide: "5 Best Secrets to Eliminating Stress and Worry"**

**Free Bonus "Claim Your Guide" Below For Your Bonus:**

https://success321.leadpages.co/freebodymindsoul/